stay healthy

365 Days of Veteran Affirmations

To Conquer PTSD, Create Growth and Reach Your Potential

By John H Davis
Author of *Combat To College*
Afterward by Dr. Jessie Virga, USN

As veterans we face unique challenges when it comes to our mental health. The military isn't easy on the body, mind, or soul. As veterans we have higher rates of negative things, we die earlier, drink more, have higher divorce rates and face more trauma than the average American. Nobody said the veteran journey was painless or stress free.

The internal conversations we have with ourselves in our own minds have a tremendous impact on the quality of our lives. Negativity is a normal part of life and there's no ignoring it, every veteran has been through stress and transition issues. Life is full of tragedies and veteran lives even more so. Creating a successful post-military life and finding professional and personal success is no simple task.

Every veteran has to stand guard at the gate of their mind and be selective about what gets through. Toxicity can hijack our mental algorithm if we let our guard down. What's fed into this algorithm creates our mindset and reality. It's time veterans work as hard for positivity as the world seems to work for negativity. In the absence of light, darkness takes over.

I've struggled on my veteran journey. I've been to war and jail, have a pair of divorces, and been addicted to alcohol and pills. I've been to brothels in Bangkok and have spent hundreds of hours in tattoo parlors because the pain made me feel alive. I've been to rock bottom and bounced back. In my own healing, when I practice daily affirmations, my life improves. I get happier, gain greater focus and accomplish more. Proverbs states, "As You Think, So You Are." Taking control of your mind leads to amazing things.

Affirmations are a powerful tool to uplift veterans. That doesn't mean daily affirmations are a magic pill. But if you've been in the military, you've heard the phrase "Fake it till you make it." Affirmations help combat PTSD, build self-confidence and develop emotional resilience. We've been trained to take care of our brothers and sisters in arms and have been ready to make the ultimate sacrifice for our friends.

Veterans believe in service to others and now it's time to shift our mindset to serve ourselves. Self-care is important for everyone, but especially veterans as our population shrinks over time. Every day veterans die and fewer join, we're becoming an endangered species. You're not only important to your family and community but to the very soul of our nation.

A veteran affirmation routine doesn't have to be complicated or take much time. Use this resource in whatever way works best for you. There's one a day to keep it straightforward, you can read them, write them down or say them out loud. Doing them in the morning to motivate yourself and clear your head is the most effective. For too long I relied on the VA and medication to heal me with abysmal results. Veterans have to step up and be the directors of our own therapy and healthcare to find out what works for us. Affirmations are part of that and saying them daily will promote a happier, healthier and more successful life.

The law of attraction suggests thinking positive thoughts brings positivity and dwelling on negativity brings more negativity. Whatever you focus on you're going to attract and draw into your life. Veterans have a tendency to use dark humor and sarcasm; it's how we cope with the difficulties of military life. That leads to an

"Embrace the suck" mentality that can drag us down. The military leaves a scar on everyone who serves and impacts all of us, nobody who comes out the military is the same person that went in.

Your mind is the only true thing you completely own. It's the most important possession any veteran has, yes, even more so than your rifle. That six inches between your ears is your territory and it requires a strong defense. There are always enemies, toxicity, negativity, and saboteurs trying to sneak inside. Affirmations help keep the insurgents out of your mental territory. This book provides a tool for veterans to overcome our PTSD and unique challenges. By embracing our veteran spirit, we can unlock our full potential to lead the lives post-service that we deserve.

Throughout this book you'll find 365 affirmations written directly for veterans. The veteran life can be a challenge for even the strongest among us and daily affirmations are one tool in life's battles. Through these daily veteran affirmations you will:

- Boost your emotional health
- Increase self-confidence
- Embrace your inner warrior
- Build mental strength
- Improve focus and set goals
- Promote healing
- Achieve your goals

This journal came to be after a personal coaching experience where I wrote thirty days of affirmations specifically for one veteran and his life. Those thirty days of affirmations he shared with his PTSD support group, they utilized them and experienced growth. This book is for that PTSD group, all the veterans struggling out there and the veterans trying to reach for their potential post-service.

Keep putting one foot in front of the other. Make today, this week, this month and this year the best yet by combining these affirmations with healthy living.

Let's go.

Contents

January 09

February 17

March 25

April 33

May 41

June 49

July 57

August 65

September 73

October 81

November 89

December 96

Conclusion 104

Afterward 106

More by the Author 108

January

> "The most important possession you have is your name – Never dishonor it."

David H. McNerney, United States Army
Medal of Honor

Word of the Month: Commitment

The beginning of any year provides a fresh opportunity for a new start. January is the perfect time for new goals and a prime time to kick off new habits. If you think back to the times when you accomplished something, you demonstrated commitment to that outcome. When you think about times you fell short of your goal, it was likely because your commitment was lacking. When veterans commit to a mission, success is possible no matter the odds.

Forget New Year's Resolutions, make New Year's Commitments. There's a difference between being interested in something and being committed to it. Lots of people are interested in being healthier, healing and making more money, but the ones that accomplish it are committed. The first resolutions were recorded into history by the Babylonians 4,000 years ago who believed whatever a person did on the first day of the year carried into the rest of it. Momentum matters on the battlefield and in life and veterans should start January strong. If you don't build momentum you'll always be starting over, use these affirmations to set the tone for the coming year.

10

JANUARY

You can make positive changes in your mindset in a month and enormous changes in your life over a year. These affirmations are the start to better mental health because veterans are at their best when they have a mission to undertake and a battle to win.

January 1st

I'm grateful for my service and what it has provided for me, the good and the bad has made me who I am. I'm proud of what I've done for my country, my community and my family.

January 2nd

I'm part of a community far larger and greater than I am. I'm on a veteran journey with fellow journeyers, I'm not alone.

January 3rd

I am a strong veteran of purpose and conviction.

January 4th

My life is not in the hands of the military anymore, it's mine to own and if I don't live it, no one else will because no one else can.

January 5th

I am a veteran and that's something to be proud of. My duty is to stay on my own path.

January 6th

Oher veterans have been through what I've been through, pain is part of the veteran life. No matter what the military has handed me, I can handle it.

Jan 7th

Every day in the military I grew smarter and stronger. I will continue to challenge myself physically and mentally.

Jan 8th

I'm going to do whatever is right in front of me. Then I'm going to do the next thing. The targets are all getting knocked down one by one.

Jan 9th

I am healthy. I am happy. I am a veteran.

Jan 10th

My service can never be taken from me. I earned the right to call myself an American veteran.

Jan 11th

My life is in my hands now, I choose where to put my attention and energy.

Jan 12th

I will take a break when I need it. I will breathe, I will keep breathing. I will do what I have been trained to do and meet my life head on.

JANUARY

Jan 13th

My commitment to winning my personal battles will not waver.

Jan 14th

My military challenges have given me the strength to get through any situation.

Jan 15th

My training is never complete.[1]

Jan 16th

I will commit to exercise and living healthy. In the military physical training was important and I will take that mentality into my civilian life.

Jan 17th

I'm a strong veteran, being weak is dangerous.

January 18th

The military tested my limits, I will continue to push them in my civilian life.

---

1 Navy Seal Creed

January 19th
My life is my mission, I will fight and win. Completing my mission is inspiring to other veterans.

January 20th
I release relationships that are toxic to me. I'm committed to healthy relationships.

January 21st
I will be a model citizen and a proud veteran in my community.

January 22nd
I embrace my veteran status with pride.

January 23rd
People I've served with can count on me to be there for them.

January 24th
I will be the solution, never the problem.

January 25th
I will not seek out conflict but I won't shy away from them.

January 26th

I am a veteran with honor.

January 27th

I'm confident in my ability to continue making a positive difference in the world.

January 28th

I'm a veteran leader in my community, using my respect and influence to make a positive impact.

January 29th

I'm trained and ready for dangerous situations. I can save lives. I'll run into danger if need be.

January 30th

I'll stand tall above the competition; I will be the example.

January 31st

I accept all challenges involved in veteran life.

16   JANUARY

Monthly Reflection

What were my monthly victories? What went well for me?

_____
_____
_____
_____

How can I make my habits better for next month?

_____
_____
_____
_____

What lessons did I learn this month?

_____
_____
_____
_____

February

> *"I always remember the day I took the oath to support and defend the Constitution of the United States. That really meant something to me."*

John W. Finn, United States Navy
Medal of Honor

Word of the Month: Courage

Raising your right hand and swearing to uphold and defend the constitution of the United States is a courageous act. Veterans are brave people, and we need to remember where we're from and what we've accomplished. Courage gives us the ability to act despite our fears. Courage isn't something you either have or don't have, it's something that can be strengthened. Courage isn't the norm for everyone, but it is for veterans.

Aristotle called courage the first virtue, because it makes all the other virtues possible. We call upon on our veteran courage during life and death moments, but courage can also mean the willingness to keep fighting despite the odds. To keep showing up, working on our PTSD, and striving to be better than yesterday. This February, step into your courage by getting outside your comfort zone. Courage begets courage so take a stand this month for yourself, for others and embrace your convictions. If you don't act courageously on what you believe to be right, you'll find yourself living with regrets.

18

February doesn't have a lot happening, the holidays are long gone, and it can be the coldest month of the year. It can lack the optimism that January has, and Valentines Day brings up mixed emotions. You'll inspire people around you when you remain optimistic and act with confidence. Courage is about taking calculated risks and seizing opportunities. We all fear failure, but courage is the fuel you need to succeed this month. Pour a little extra on and attack February and be the best version of yourself that you can be.

February 1st
Veterans who came before me have sacrificed for me, today I'll make them proud.

February 2nd
I'm going to march to my own cadence and in my own direction.

February 3rd
I will develop strength by facing my fears. I will face them again and again until I am victorious.

February 4th
My demons are not stronger than I am. I have been trained to defeat all enemies, even the enemy within.

February 5th
Each day I am stronger, more powerful and closer to my goals.

February 6th
I won't fight with one hand tied behind my back. In the military we learn half commitments lead to half results. I'll fight to not to survive, but to win.

February 7th

Nothing is permanent, not negativity, anxiety, pain or discomfort. I will remember that today and know that this too… will pass.

February 8th

I will not be retreating. I will not wave a white flag. I will win.

February 9th

I stepped into the unknown when I raised my right hand. I will continue facing civilian life with courage as I did in the military.

February 10th

I cannot meet the challenges of a veteran life without courage. I acknowledge that courage is something that can be strengthened.

February 11th

My courage is contagious to fellow veterans.

February 12th

I can heal my military pain.

February 13th

I am a determined veteran who pursues my goals with courage.

February 14th

My military training gives me confidence to deal with my obstacles today.

February 15th

I will do more, rather than less of my share.

February 16th

Failure is a part of life; I may lose a battle but I will come back and win the war.

February 17th

Conquering all obstacles, both large and small, I will never quit.[2]

February 18th

I'm a veteran, a warrior and I can protect the people I love from harm.

---

2 Marine Recon Creed

February 19th

I'm not going to stay in dark places, I'll fight through to reach the light.

February 20th

I am a talented veteran with many skills and abilities.

February 21st

I am a risk-taker, I do not fear the unknown.

February 22nd

In the most difficult of times, I'm a beacon of light for others.

February 23rd

When courage is needed, others can look to me for inspiration.

February 24th

I will conquer my PTSD, for I am a conqueror.

February 25th

I see the potential not only in myself but also my fellow veterans.

February 26th

I am a warrior every day of my life.

February 27th

I am a believer in peace through strength.

February 28th

I am a veteran and I know my worth.

24

FEBRUARY

Monthly Reflection

What were my monthly victories? What went well for me?

_____
_____
_____
_____

How can I make my habits better for next month?

_____
_____
_____
_____

What lessons did I learn this month?

_____
_____
_____
_____

365 DAYS OF VETERAN AFFIRMATIONS — BY JOHN H DAVIS

March

> *"When something needs to be done, push ahead and overcome all obstacles because there is always a way."*
>
> **Jay Zeamer Jr., United States Air Corps**
> **Medal of Honor**

Word of the Month: Leader

To be a leader worthy of following, you must first effectively lead yourself. Self-leadership is the most important type of leadership because, for better or worse, you have to be in charge of yourself. Your duty in the military is to lead others with a clearly defined mission. In civilian life you lead yourself on goals you create. Affirmations assist in providing that purpose, direction, and motivation to the person in the mirror.

There's no escaping your own thoughts and no denying that every veteran has to fight against internal enemies. But you can make your head a better place by taking control of your thoughts. Leading yourself means figuring out who you are and what you want to accomplish. It means being accountable to yourself and having your own best interests at heart. Leading yourself is trusting your judgment, remaining calm, and acting because you want to do something, not because someone told you to.

By the end of March, aim to be in a better position than you were in the beginning. Be honest about your strengths and weaknesses, take initiative and strive to be a role model. Service to others doesn't end when your uniform comes off. You're still a leader within your family, community, and the country. Live your values and embrace self-leadership this March.

March 1st

Every day provides an opportunity to use my military leadership skills.

March 2nd

In the military I wasn't fully in charge of the direction of my life. Now I am and I have to lead myself on missions of my own making.

March 3rd

I'm the leader of my own life and the star of my movie. It's going to play out the way I want it to.

March 4th

I will lead myself forward from where I find myself today. I will fight to gain ground and expand my territory.

March 5th

I've seen toxic leaders in the military. I will not be that, I will be better.

March 6th

I will forge my own path using everything the military taught me.

March 7th

I'm in command of my own life, attitude and decisions.

March 8th

I possess the leadership qualities needed to be successful.

March 9th

I am a warrior, I'm willing to do what's hard.

March 10th

I've lived by the military's rules, now I get to live by my own.

March 11th

My military values know the way, I'll trust and follow them.

March 12th

The only easy day was yesterday.[3]

March 13th

It's okay for me to show emotion.

---

[3] Navy Seal Motto

MARCH

March 14th
I lead myself everyday towards a better future.

March 15th
My feelings of anxiety and insecurity are feelings not facts.

March 16th
I will not give in to weakness, not today.

March 17th
Even the smallest steps in the right direction are still steps in the right direction.

March 18th
I defend my country and my fellow veterans with my life.

March 19th
My health and happiness are worth fighting for.

March 20th
My veteran energy makes me powerful.

March 21st

I'm open to calling for support and receiving help.

March 22nd

I represent the fighting spirit of the America.

March 23rd

If I'm feeling tired or burnt out, I'll rest and recover.

March 24th

I pledge to uphold the honor and integrity of all I am- in all I do.[4]

March 25th

I have a responsibility to protect my home and defend my fortress.

March 26th

I'm never out of the fight.[5]

---

4   Special Forces Creed, US Army
5   Navy Seal Code

March 27th

I am confident in who I am as a veteran, I stand here with power.

March 28th

I'm at peace with my military experiences, I won't apologize for being me.

March 29th

I'm going to make the healthiest choices for my mental and physical health.

Monthly Reflection

What were my monthly victories? What went well for me?

_____
_____
_____
_____

How can I make my habits better for next month?

_____
_____
_____
_____

What lessons did I learn this month?

_____
_____
_____
_____

April

"Life on this earth is short but precious. Strive to do good for others and enjoy doing it."

**Joseph C. Rodriguez, United States Army
Medal of Honor**

Word of the Month: Change

Leo Tolstoy said, "Everyone thinks of changing the world, but no one thinks of changing themselves." April marks the beginning of change in the natural world and you should be changing too. Embracing change propels veterans forward in life, refusing it leads to stagnation. The arrival of spring means new adventures. April marks the start of transformation for Mother Nature and an opportunity for you to make small changes with big payoffs.

Veterans have three distinct phases of life, before, during and after their military service. How veterans handle these transitions has a big impact on how our lives play out. Change is normal, but unsettling. There's no such thing as living your life in the same place, doing the same things around the same people. There's a story about a janitor at NASA in 1961. When JFK was touring the building, he asked the man what he was doing. The janitor responded, "Well, Mr. President, I'm helping to put a man on the moon." Regardless of our role, changing our outlook has the power to change our world.

34

When you rise to embrace a challenge, it changes you. No one is the same after serving in the military; it transforms us all. Accepting the changing nature of the world means our difficult times won't last forever. April represents hope for a better future. Allow yourself to evolve and grow this spring, it's time to embrace changes.

April 1st

I will be open to change. The military changed me and I will continue to change, to evolve and to grow. Progress requires change.

April 2nd

This is my moment to change my life. I'll embrace that change and sail confidently into uncharted waters.

April 3rd

My inner mentality creates my outer world.

April 4th

The first step is to square myself away. If I find myself out of step, I will not criticize or judge others.

April 5th

I'll say yes to new opportunities and experiences.

April 6th

My family and friends might not always change with me but that's not going to stop me from embracing positive change in my life. Not everyone is going to be who I want them to be.

April 7th
I am a guardian of freedom and the American way of life.[6]

April 8th
I refuse to let my PTSD rule me.

April 9th
The military trained me to be adaptable, I will continue to adapt and overcome.

April 10th
Even when I'm tired, I'll continue to put one foot in front of the other.

April 11th
I believe in my training and capabilities.

April 12th
I am committed to excellence in all things.

---

6   Soldier's Creed, Army

April 13th

Strength is in my nature; victory is my destiny.

April 14th

I don't have to live in dark places, there is no growth for me there.

April 15th

I want to see change in the country, I will be the change I wish to see in America.

April 16th

I give myself permission to serve myself and my own needs.

April 17th

I always have my own six.

April 18th

I seek opportunities to lift up my fellow veterans.

April 19th

I served with honor in the military and live with integrity as a civilian.

April 20th

I am growing, learning and changing for the better. I can feel it.

April 21st

I'm not what happened to me in my military past, I'll create the future I deserve.

April 22nd

I am a warrior, but I am also a peacemaker. I can find solutions to problems.

April 23rd

I don't compare myself to other veterans.

April 24th

The mantle of a powerful veteran is mine to bear.

April 25th

I am my country's strength in war and her deterrent in peace.[7]

April 26th

I don't have to carry everything. I can shed some of my military pain from my rucksack when it grows heavy.

April 27th

My veteran spirit is unbreakable.

April 28th

I'm dedicated to moving forward towards the battle, towards the sound of the guns today.

April 29th

I don't need to be perfect, being the veteran I am is enough.

April 30th

I'll ask for forgiveness if I wrong someone.

---

[7] Infantryman's Creed, Army

Monthly Reflection

What were my monthly victories? What went well for me?

_____
_____
_____
_____

How can I make my habits better for next month?

_____
_____
_____
_____

What lessons did I learn this month?

_____
_____
_____
_____

May

"I came when I was called and I did the best I could."

**John D. Hawk, United States Army
Medal of Honor**

Word of the Month: Creativity

It's up to veterans to lead our own healing and therapy and that means getting creative. Sometimes the first few things we try in our healing don't work and we have to think outside the box. Creativity keeps you engaged in your own life and doing meaningful activities. There are many ways to be creative, you don't need to play the piano or paint a picture. Military service can dull our creative edge, every veteran has the potential to infuse more creativity into their lives. We wear the same thing day after day, eat the same food, and after a while serving can feel like groundhogs day.

Losing yourself in some sort of activity is going to reduce your stress levels and helps you relax. There's something for every veteran, you can journal, play make-believe with your kids, play basketball, photography, cook or reorganize a room. Creativity is energizing and allows us to express our unique selves. This May reject living on autopilot and incorporate creativity into your day to day.

Writing helped me build confidence because I learned my failures were part of the process. Creativity isn't just for hippies or artsy type people, it's in everything. You can be creative at work and

42

be more productive and effective. There's a reason why so many PTSD programs push creativity on veterans to discover purpose, meaning and beauty. Open up your mind this May, ask questions and challenge yourself to be creative.

May 1st

I will seek out what inspires me. I will find things that light a fire within.

May 2nd

I added value to the country through my service and now I will add value to my own life.

May 3rd

I'm capable of creating, I have creative power.

May 4th

There's so much I can do to influence and create my future. I'll take advantage of opportunities.

May 5th

I have no desire to live a half-life. I want everything that this world has to offer.

May 6th

The more I give to my community, the more I get from my community.

May 7th

I will encourage, support and congratulate myself and my creative spirit today.

May 8th

In the military, much of what it offers you is what you offer it. Civilian life isn't that different, you get what you give.

May 9th

I will not wait for inspiration to find me, I will take action.

May 10th

I will find creative ways to help my fellow veterans, I will pay it forward.

May 11th

I will place my integrity first, service before self and strive for excellence.[8]

May 12th

I can make room in my life now for spontaneity and fun.

---

[8] Air Force Core Values

May 13th

I'm needed in my community.

May 14th

When I fail, I'll hold my head high. Honor is in my DNA.

May 15th

My life is a source of inspiration for younger veterans.

May 16th

I'll thank another veteran for their service today.

May 17th

My veteran friendships are deep and meaningful.

May 18th

I am not my PTSD. PTSD is an experience I am going through.

May 19th

I will evolve as a veteran, creator and person.

May 20th

If knocked down, I will get back up, every time.[9]

May 21st

I am a strong leader in my family and community.

May 22nd

I am a defender of this country, in uniform or not.

May 23rd

My PTSD is real but so is my veteran resilience.

May 24th

I will face my challenges head on, with all my training and abilities and emerge victorious.

May 25th

I am a trailblazing veteran, committed to creating new opportunities for myself.

---

9   Navy Seal Creed

May 26th

I am faithful to a proud heritage.[10]

May 27th

I am committed to creating a better future for myself and fellow veterans.

May 28th

I will be true to myself as well as my military values.

May 29th

The bond of American veterans is unbreakable.

May 30th

I'm grateful for my military abilities and will use them to help myself and others.

May 31st

I'm a professional and believe in honor, respect, and devotion to duty.[11]

---

10   Airman's Creed, Air Force
11   Coast Guard Values

48 MAY

Monthly Reflection

What were my monthly victories? What went well for me?

_____
_____
_____
_____

How can I make my habits better for next month?

_____
_____
_____
_____

What lessons did I learn this month?

_____
_____
_____
_____

June

> "Millions have served in the military and made sacrifices, and most have gone unrecognized. We owe a special thanks to all veterans and those on active duty"

George E. Wahlen, United States Army
Medal of Honor

Word of the Month: Honesty

Today's world is overflowing with mistruths and disinformation from internet culture and corporate media. The veil has been pulled away and now there are Americans who have lost faith in the government, news, and institutions. Veterans have a responsibility to stand firm in our values and live honestly with the world and ourselves. Veterans don't dance around the truth and aren't concerned about offending. Being truthful comes naturally to veterans. It's simple, but that doesn't mean it's easy.

Honesty is a way to get more of what you want; veterans know directness equals results. Speak up this June about your desires and goals to both others and yourself. Living honestly provides peace and mitigates negative characteristics like greed, disloyalty, and hypocrisy. Servicemembers get their values drilled into them from boot camp onward and we can't forget those lessons. Prioritizing an honest life is the best way to keep toxic people away from you. Dishonest people steer clear from straightforward truth tellers. Embrace personal honesty, especially when it's difficult and get real with yourself. We've witnessed the importance of honesty degrade across American society in recent years. Lying used to be one of the worst offenses a person could do, now we encounter it every day.

I lied in my past because I wanted to be seen as the person I was trying to be, instead of who I actually was. I lied about everything from how much I bench pressed to lying to my therapist about my mental health. Embracing honesty means occasionally being vulnerable. Healthy and long-lasting relationships have a foundation in honesty, relationships built on lies don't last. We learn lessons by being honest, it can be a challenge to tell the truth or confess to personal mistakes. This June, make it a priority to live honestly, discard bullshit and love who you are.

June 1st

PTSD grows in the dark, I will be honest today with myself and those that care about me.

June 2nd

I am willing to live with harsh truths over comforting lies. I have accepted the things I cannot change and changed the things I can.

June 3rd

I will search for truth within myself and share it with the world.

June 4th

I will not be manipulated by others.

June 5th

I recognize every day I struggle against demons, but the battle is only lost if I stop fighting.

June 6th

Never shall I forget the principles I accepted to become a veteran. Honor, teamwork, integrity and courage.

June 7th
When I feel stress today I will do things to combat it. I will take a walk, listen to music or do what brings me peace during anxious moments.

June 8th
Honesty is my roadmap for my journey through my post-military life.

June 9th
I can't be a veteran and not be a little crazy.

June 10th
I am more disciplined than those around me, I will use that to my advantage.

June 11th
I am an American warrior, and I can handle this.

June 12th
I am what a powerful veteran looks like.

June 13th

I will not bring shame upon myself or the forces.[12]

June 14th

I thank myself for my service.

June 15th

I add value to the lives of my fellow veterans and my country.

June 16th

There are no battles I cannot win.

June 17th

I will push through my PTSD so that my struggles today will become my strengths tomorrow.

June 18th

I'm an unstoppable force. My enemies don't stand a chance.

June 19th

I have answered my nation's call when others did not.

---

12   Special Forces Creed, Army

June 20th

There's nothing I can't handle, defeat or kill.

June 21st

I am a veteran, and I will fight until victory is achieved.

June 22nd

I am striving to be the best veteran and person I can be.

June 23rd

Like the veterans who came before me, I will not back down from adversity or superior odds.

June 24th

I am a role model for civilians in difficult situations.

June 25th

I'm trained to advance, destroy my enemies and accomplish my mission.

June 26th

I am an expert and I am a professional.[13]

June 27th

My veteran grit can overcome any obstacle.

June 28th

I'll fight forwhat what's right. I'll choose the harder right over the easier wrong.

June 29th

I am dedicated to a life of patriotic purpose.

June 30th

I am influential in my community; people respect my service.

---

[13] Soldiers Creed, Army

Monthly Reflection

What were my monthly victories? What went well for me?

_____

_____

_____

_____

How can I make my habits better for next month?

_____

_____

_____

_____

What lessons did I learn this month?

_____

_____

_____

_____

July

> "We don't have problems, just solutions. Drive yourself, lead others and never offend."

**Eugene B. Fluckey, United States Navy
Medal of Honor**

Word of the Month: Passion

When I became a civilian my life lacked the passion I was used to in the military. The military gave me a deep sense of purpose and I felt inspired serving my country with my friends. When I got out of the military, nothing appeared to fill that gap I felt in my soul. Our passion and commitment to the military gives us the strength to overcome challenging obstacles and difficult circumstances. We were passionate about the people we served with and the causes we fought for. When veterans live with passion, we are unstoppable.

Discovering and living with passion post-service isn't a simple task. Pursuing your passions doesn't always guarantee career success. Being passionate about something doesn't mean someone's going to pay you to do it. Nobody's offered to pay me to drink tequila on a beach yet. Living a passionate life isn't about employment, it's about enriching your soul and boosting your mental health. Passion creates optimism and a willingness to fail while learning from those experiences.

Pursuing our passions is energizing, doing things we love feels good. While serving in the military, we spend years obeying our leaders, but it's a different story when we are free to pursue our own passions. A passionate life is a fun life, veterans don't have to be so serious all the time. A veteran life isn't meant to be a boring life, seek excitement this July. Passion doesn't come overnight, but once it does it's contagious. When you live with passion it inspires positivity, courage, and focus.

July 1st

Today I'll have fun. I'll laugh today. I fought for freedom and I'm going to enjoy it.

July 2nd

I will find my passion. I'll enjoy it to challenge and nourish my veteran spirit.

July 3rd

I'm worthy of all the things America has to offer.

July 4th

I'm pursuing progress, not perfection. The military isn't perfect, I can't expect perfection out of myself but I can be better.

July 5th

My time and what I do with it is important to me. I've given enough of my time to the military, training and deployments. I won't throw any more time away.

July 6th

I grew from my military challenges, I'll grow from my civilian ones as well.

July 7th

I was energized in the military during training I enjoyed. I'll rekindle that energy through my passions.

July 8th

I won't let go of the things that I'm passionate about. I deserve to enjoy my hobbies in civilian life.

July 9th

I'm worthy of all my veteran benefits.

July 10th

I'll share my passions with other veterans. We deserve to come together and build community.

July 11th

If all I see is closed doors, I won't despair. I will kick them down.

July 12th

I will do an act of kindness today for a fellow veteran.

July 13th
Part of my veteran journey is helping other veterans. Part of my healing is helping other veterans heal.

July 14th
I'll tell my veteran story to the people I love. I want them to understand me.

July 15th
I've been through the fire and come out stronger.

July 16th
I have earned the right to be happy.

July 17th
I'm there for my veteran brothers and sisters.

July 18th
When conflict arises, I'll stand my ground and won't back down.

July 19th
Bad experiences are part of life, it's okay for me to have a bad day.

July 20th
I stayed alive today. I'll stay alive tomorrow.

July 21st
I'll call my fellow veterans for support if I need it.

July 22nd
Veterans are not victims, I'm far from a victim.

July 23rd
I'm passionate about veteran causes.

July 24th
Being disciplined comes naturally to me.

July 25th
The best things I've done, aren't the best things I'll ever do. I have a promising future.

July 26th
I still have an important mission to accomplish.

July 27th
My life matters to other veterans.

July 28th
I have the power and discipline to create personal success.

July 29th
The veteran life is an adventure.

July 30th
I will never surrender thought I may be the last.[14]

July 31st
The military has no power over me anymore.

---

14 Special Forces Creed, US Army

Monthly Reflection

What were my monthly victories? What went well for me?

_____
_____
_____
_____

How can I make my habits better for next month?

_____
_____
_____
_____

What lessons did I learn this month?

_____
_____
_____
_____

August

> "Honor those who have served our country, especially those who made the ultimate sacrifice. Educate future generations about the price paid for the freedom we enjoy in America the beautiful."

Freeman V. Horner, United States Army
Medal of Honor

Word of the Month: Peace

Veterans can often feel more comfortable at war than at peace. Peace isn't something veterans can snap their fingers and magically receive. Embracing mental and physical peace helps veterans live in the moment and not stress about the past. Welcoming peace pushes anxiety, sleeplessness, and PTSD away. Inner peace helps veterans focus on what's truly important in life and not get caught up in minor things and most things are minor things. After the things America's veterans have seen and done, we deserve peace on the home front.

When you have peace, you trust yourself and your decisions. Veterans have a tendency to be too hard on ourselves, we learn in the military mistakes can mean life and death. There's no mastering peace for veterans, but our lives should be more satisfying than combative. It goes beyond our emotional health into the physical realm. Stress is as much of a killer for veterans after service than our enemies are on the battlefield.

Peace is a journey, not a destination. Veterans know there are times when battles are necessary but not with the person in the mirror. Sometimes, without an enemy to fight veterans risk going to war with themselves. The cost of a life overflowing with conflict is increased PTSD, a lack of purpose and decreased mental health. Pay attention to what and how you think this month and seek peace.

August 1st

I will not live in anger or resentment. The military focuses outward but now I will focus inward and seek peace.

August 2nd

Denying my problems doesn't make them go away, solving them does.

August 3rd

I will separate my military past from my present. It will not dictate my future.

August 4th

The soul of a warrior isn't something that ever goes away. A fighter will always live inside me.

August 5th

I'll take a deep breath and reset when I need to.

August 6th

I can let my guard down. I don't need to be on edge or hyperalert today.

August 7th

I can't live my life backwards; my military past is in the past. I can live in each moment today; I will be present in my life today.

August 8th

I learned emotional control in the military. I will regulate my emotions today and not let them dictate my mood.

August 9th

I will detach from those who bring negativity into my life.

August 10th

I'll set personal boundaries whenever necessary to protect my peace.

August 11th

I live with honor in both word and deed.

August 12th

My core values are honor, courage, and commitment.[15]

---

15   Navy and Marine Corps Values

August 13th
I'll pay attention today to my military triggers.

August 14th
I don't have everything that I want but I do appreciate what I have.

August 15th
I'll go to war to create peace.

August 16th
I am a warrior and a member of a team.[16]

August 17th
I have control over my mind, thoughts and sword.

August 18th
I'm powerful enough to overcome anything.

August 19th
I'm not alone, other veterans are with me in spirit.

---

16 Soldier's Creed, Army

August 20th
I am not in America, I am America.

August 21st
Every hardship enriches my veteran soul.

August 22nd
I'm connected to a greater purpose, I am leaving behind a legacy.

August 23rd
I'm connected to American warriors past, present, and future.

August 24th
When I don't react to things, I feel peace.

August 25th
I pay tribute to fallen veterans by living a good life.

August 26th
I'm proud of my military achievements.

August 27th
I'm motivated to help my fellow veterans.

August 28th
I am an unbeatable warrior, trained by the most powerful military the world has ever known.

August 29th
The strength of past generations of veterans flows through me.

August 30th
My enemies are not as strong, well-trained, or capable as I am.

August 31st
My military values and personal actions inspire others.

Monthly Reflection

What were my monthly victories? What went well for me?

_____
_____
_____
_____

How can I make my habits better for next month?

_____
_____
_____
_____

What lessons did I learn this month?

_____
_____
_____
_____

September

"We are extremely lucky to live in a nation where the dreams for our lives can be fulfilled."

**Melvin E. Biddle, United States Army
Medal of Honor**

Word of the Month: Gratitude

Gratitude is strongly and consistently linked with greater happiness for veterans. Taking a moment here and there to acknowledge what we are thankful for helps veterans feel optimistic in the face of challenges. It isn't always easy to be grateful, some days suck from start to finish. However even on our worst days, if you look hard enough you can always find something to be grateful for. For starters we should always be grateful for our service because it forged us into who we are.

Fortunately, gratitude is a muscle that we can build. People who practice gratitude have stronger immune systems, exercise more, sleep better, and are less bothered by day-to-day aches and pains. Psychologically veterans who engage in gratitude experience higher levels of positive emotions including joy and happiness. Socially, veterans who are grateful volunteer more, have stronger communities, and are less lonely and isolated. Living with gratitude doesn't mean life is perfect but there are always things to have appreciation for.

This September be grateful and embrace the present moment. Don't take the little things for granted. Reflect on a conversation with a good friend, a walk outdoors, a good movie, or even a good meal. Gratitude puts up a defense against negative emotions like jealousy and regret that can build in people managing PTSD. Living gratefully is essential in fostering and building strong relationships, uplifting our mood, and combating PTSD.

September 1st

Today and every day I'm grateful for the men and women that have laid down their lives for me.

September 2nd

The military wasn't easy, but I didn't sign up for easy. I want challenges.

September 3rd

I appreciate the benefits I have today because of the veterans that came before me.

September 4th

I am a missile locked onto my goals.

September 5th

I'll live the way of the warrior.

September 6th

I'm proud of what I've done and I'll do more.

September 7th
My service to America is far from over.

September 8th
Veterans are the backbone of America.

September 9th
Not every veteran makes it out of the military alive. I'm grateful to be here.

September 10th
In the military I was surrounded by people who were on my team. I can create a new team of people who want me to achieve my goals.

September 11th
Today I remember the lives lost on 9/11. I also remember how America came together in the face of adversity.

September 12th
Day after day, I'm living with honor and integrity.

SEPTEMBER

September 13th

I stand ready, today and every day. If my country or my brothers and sisters in arms need me, I'll be there.[17]

September 14th

Honor is my touchstone.

September 15th

When I need support, I will call on my fellow veterans.

September 16th

I am a veteran with gratitude and appreciation for my military experiences.

September 17th

I am a confident warrior, I live with gratitude for my military mentors.

September 18th

I celebrate with my fellow veterans; we survived the military.

---

17 Cadet Creed, Army

September 19th

My fellow veterans are important to me. I'm important to my fellow veterans.

September 20th

I intend to live this day with gratitude in honor of the men and women who have died for my freedom.

September 21st

I'm giving my family the strong, healthy veteran they deserve.

September 22nd

I shall endeavor to be a model citizen in the community in which I live.[18]

September 23rd

I won't look for the easy way out. My journey isn't supposed to be easy.

September 24th

Even when I'm outside my comfort zone I'm comfortable, I've been here before.

---

18 Coast Guard Creed

September 25th

I am happy for the success of my fellow veterans.

September 26th

I will do my duty, wherever and whatever that may be.

September 27th

I live in the real world, not on social media.

September 28th

I provide leadership, stability, and continuity during war and peace.[19]

September 29th

I've made it through worse days and I'm still here.

September 30th

I am my nation's sword and shield.

---

19 Army Civilian Corps Creed

Monthly Reflection

What were my monthly victories? What went well for me?

_____
_____
_____
_____

How can I make my habits better for next month?

_____
_____
_____
_____

What lessons did I learn this month?

_____
_____
_____
_____

October

> *"Our freedom, envied the world over, was attained at great personal sacrifice – we cannot allow it to wither away through apathy."*

Thomas J. Hudner, United States Army
Medal of Honor

Word of the Month: Ambition

Ambition is what fuels veterans to reach their potential post-service. It's that inner drive that helps you stay focused on your goals, it's a desire to succeed no matter the costs. Ambition is complex and often looked at in a negative light by underachievers. But ambition is exactly what propels veterans forward to achieve great things and a lack of ambition will hold us back. Ambitious veterans are the ones willing to put in the work to accomplish their goals.

Veterans are wired to thrive when we feel appropriately challenged. Having ambition leads us to those challenges that we need to reach our potential. We enjoy victories and understand the process of winning isn't always easy. The military is a competitive environment full of ambitious people but civilian life can dull that warrior edge. The military doesn't give out participation trophies, the civilian world does. Being ambitious emphasizes the need for personal betterment and a disciplined approach to life, which comes naturally to veterans. It's a continuous cycle geared towards self-improvement.

Finding your ambition gives you a clear path forward. Being ambitious builds your confidence when you know what you want. Let your personal ambition guide your life choices this October. Ambition is the enemy of complacency. Being ambitious this month will teach veterans life lessons about strategic planning, learning from setbacks, and determination. When others can't see or understand your vision, or don't believe in you, lean into your ambition.

October 1st

My military challenges didn't destroy me, they showed me how strong I am.

October 2nd

Even as I age, I'll retain the warrior mindset.

October 3rd

Every mistake I've made has taught me something. My veteran wisdom is something that's been earned.

October 4th

Forever shall I strive to maintain the tremendous reputation of those who went before me.[20]

October 5th

I don't compare myself to other veterans, I'm on my own journey.

October 6th

My battles require armor, I'll surround myself with veteran support systems and people that have my six.

---

20 Marine Recon Creed

October 7th

My voice must be heard.

October 8th

I view my PTSD as a challenge to be overcome.

October 9th

I chose to be a fighter and I'll continue fighting.

October 10th

I'm open to healing, even when it's a journey.

October 11th

I'm still a force to be reckoned with. My training is ingrained into me. I can shoot, move and communicate.

October 12th

I'm prepared for the next battle.

October 13th

I couldn't say no in the military, now I'm saying no to things that don't serve me.

October 14th

The military is the biggest risk of all, I'm not afraid to take risks and go into the fire.

October 15th

I am trustworthy, others know they can rely on me.

October 16th

I will not fail my fellow veterans.

October 17th

My military values push me in the direction of my goals.

October 18th

I will always keep myself mentally alert, physically strong and morally straight and I will shoulder more than my share of the task whatever it may be, one-hundred-percent and then some.[21]

October 19th

I am the embodiment of strength and determination.

---

21   Ranger Creed, Army

October 20th
I can handle pressure easily, I have before and will again.

October 21st
I celebrate my service and the service of my fellow veterans. Freedom is a cost that we've paid together.

October 22nd
If the military didn't break me, my PTSD doesn't stand a chance.

October 23rd
I will use my success to give back to the veteran community.

October 24th
I have a deep gratitude for my military friends that aren't here anymore.

October 25th
Doubt has no place in my mind.

October 26th
The military and life has knocked me down, but I will rise again and again.

October 27th
I'm grateful for the people who are currently serving.

October 28th
I will not shrink from adversity, I am a gladiator. I'll step confidently into the arena.

October 29th
I feel good to be alive and be a veteran. I've done things with my life.

October 30th
I'm guided by the wisdom of military heroes, who sacrificed for my freedoms.

October 31st
I will not be defeated, for I am a strong and powerful veteran.

Monthly Reflection

What were my monthly victories? What went well for me?

_____
_____
_____
_____

How can I make my habits better for next month?

_____
_____
_____
_____

What lessons did I learn this month?

_____
_____
_____
_____

November

> "To be an American comes with many rights, privileges, and responsibilities. It is our duty to honor, defend and preserve them for future generations."

Richard A. Pittman, United States Marine Corps
Medal of Honor

Word of the Month: Persistence

There are times when as a veteran it feels like the world is against you and there's moments where we all feel like giving up. But the veteran experience is not for quitters, we win when we keep fighting. Benjamin Franklin said, "Energy and persistence conquer all things." Many people believe talent or luck are what creates success but high performing people embrace persistence. If you take an axe and hit a tree a thousand times in different places, nothing will happen. When you take that axe and persistently hit the tree in the same place a thousand times the tree will fall.

As long as you persist and keep trying, there's no failure. There are a lot of benefits to being persistent this November. Persistence can lead to expertise as you try again and again until you succeed, it sets an example for people that look up to you. Nothing great is ever done without a measure of persistence. People are bound to judge you based on your consistency, put in the extra effort this month to be consistent. There are many obstacles on our path to success: fear, distractions, criticism, and indecision. Persistence conquers them all.

There can be no persistence without a goal or a desire. Identify what you want to achieve, make a plan and build yourself a support system to get there. It's a smart idea to surround yourself with good company while you work towards your accomplishments. Whatever your goal may be, you aren't going to be successful on the first try or probably the second. When that feeling of discouragement creeps in, tap into your veteran persistence to keep going. Don't give up on your goals this November, be persistent and fight through to your objective.

November 1st

I'm in this for the long haul. I'm committed to my success and contributing to the country long after I'm out of uniform.

November 2nd

I'm still my brothers and sisters keeper.

November 3rd

I'm trained to fight through pain, to push through and to be victorious.

November 4th

Every veteran makes mistakes, what's important is I keep pushing on.

November 5th

I'm proud of my military achievements. They didn't come easy.

November 6th

The military was hard on my body, I'm going to take care better care of it.

November 7th

My veteran persistence will win every battle.

November 8th

I'm aware of my scars and proud of my past.

November 9th

In every fight, I'm going to go the distance.

November 10th

My persistence will conquer all resistance.

November 11th

I have a hunger for betterment and success. I owe it to my fellow veterans.

November 12th

Now I serve others and the country my way. But I still serve.

November 13th

I have the power of veteran endurance. I don't stop when I'm tired, I stop when I win.

November 14th
I am allowing my veteran body to heal.

November 15th
Veterans deserve respect, I deserve respect.

November 16th
I will never forget who I am or what I represent.[22]

November 17th
I was not trained to give up. Every day presents an opportunity to prove myself.

November 18th
My ability to win my personal wars is unlimited.

November 19th
I am a beacon of strength for my fellow veterans and my country.

---

22 Marine NCO Creed

November 20th

I trained for hardship, I'll tap into that today. I'm ready for this.

November 21st

I fight my PTSD with persistence. Some days it may get the better of me, but in the long run it's no match for my power.

November 22nd

Warrior energy courses through me.

November 23rd

I won't be a victim of my military past. I'm stronger because of my experiences.

November 24th

My family looks to me as a role model, I will make them proud.

November 25th

I'm proud of my identity as an American veteran. It's a badge of honor.

November 30th

My pain is real, but it won't define me or defeat me.

NOVEMBER

Monthly Reflection

What were my monthly victories? What went well for me?

_____
_____
_____
_____

How can I make my habits better for next month?

_____
_____
_____
_____

What lessons did I learn this month?

_____
_____
_____
_____

December

> "Go with honor, return with honor. That is America in action"

George E. Day, United States Air Force
Medal of Honor

Word of the Month: Resilient

Being resilient is what gives veterans the emotional strength to cope with PTSD. Resiliency gives us the psychological strength we need to deal with the veteran experience, stress, and hardship. Resiliency doesn't make problems go away or cure PTSD but it can give you the power to keep going. Harnessing your veteran resilience this December is going to help you recover and bounce back from the setbacks you've faced this year.

Military life requires veterans to be resilient to withstand the difficulties of service. Civilian life requires a different kind of resiliency, in the military there is group and unit resiliency, you're strong because of the people around you. Civilian life requires you to build individual resiliency and that takes practice and time. Veterans face all types of adversity, both in and out of uniform. People who lack resiliency are more likely to suffer more from PTSD, feel overwhelmed, and fall into unhealthy coping strategies. To increase your personal resiliency, seek to reframe setbacks with a different perspective this December. Tap into positive emotions, use the daily affirmations, and be optimistic about the future.

DECEMBER

Veterans are survivors. We survived everything the military threw at us, but civilian life presents a different battle. To make it through we need to be resilient. The VA, relationships, finances, losses of family and loved ones, sicknesses will all take its toll. Your veteran resiliency gives you the strength to attack your PTSD and problems head on. This December close out your year strong by focusing what's in your control.

December 1st

My strength is unmatched, and I will continue to use it to help others.

December 2nd

Commitment to the path of resiliency is a commitment to myself. I won't procrastinate.

December 3rd

I've fought to get this far. It hasn't always been easy but I'm still here. I'll still be here tomorrow.

December 4th

I'm proud of the contributions veterans have made to society.

December 5th

I may have to fight the same battle more than once to win it.

December 6th

Sometimes just surviving the day is enough.

December 7th
My PTSD will not hijack my life.

December 8th
I will continue to use my training and values to make the world a better place.

December 9th
My veteran resolve is unyielding.

December 10th
I'm going to emerge victorious and more resilient from this situation.

December 11th
People have fought for me, and I have fought for others.

December 12th
I love the possibilities and freedoms I have in civilian life.

December 13th
I survived the military; I'll survive whatever life throws at me.

December 14th
My PTSD might knock me down, but I'll keep getting up.

December 15th
My love for my fellow veterans fuels me.

December 16th
America is a better place because of me and my friends.

December 17th
I'm still fighting for a just cause in my civilian life.

December 18th
I am a true warrior, and I will fight for those I love until my last breath.

December 19th
Veterans are stronger together, I'll reach out to a fellow veteran today.

December 20th
I will not let civilian setbacks discourage me; I'll use them as motivation to work harder.

December 21st

Always I fight on… through the foe, to the objective, to triumph over all.[23]

December 22nd

I am a hero in my own right.

December 23rd

I believe in my potential to continue to make a difference in the world.

December 24th

The military taught me to not give up, despite superior odds. I'll apply that mentality to my life today.

December 25th

I am a symbol of strength in a country that needs it.

December 26th

My mind is my weapon in civilian life as my rife was in the military. I'll use it to win.

---

23   Infantryman's Creed, Army

December 27th

I am a valuable member of the veteran community and American society.

December 28th

Asking for help or calling for support is a good thing.

December 29th

Like in the military, I'm always learning.

December 30th

I take full advantage of my military benefits.

December 31st

I will stick with my journey of growth; tomorrow is a new beginning and I'll be here for it. I close out this year in victory and positivity.

DECEMBER

Monthly Reflection

What were my monthly victories? What went well for me?

How can I make my habits better for next month?

What lessons did I learn this month?

Conclusion

Mastering your thoughts can yield incredible results for veterans. Negative thoughts are impossible to totally eliminate but counteracting them is possible using these affirmations. Like the military or anything else, consistency is the key to victory. Being consistent with affirmations, however you choose to use them will benefit your life and mental health.

Affirmations aren't magic, they're one tool for your toolbox. More of a treatment than a cure for PTSD. I do believe that our thoughts create energies and that positive thoughts attract positive energy. In the same manner, I think negative thoughts create negative energy. Veterans lean towards negative thoughts with dark humor and an embracing the suck mentality and that's why affirmations are especially powerful for us. I wrote this book because it didn't exist. But now it does, and I hope it helps veterans live better lives.

If you enjoyed reading this or were inspired, take a moment to leave a review on amazon and share the book with a fellow veteran. Reviews help more veterans get eyes on the book. If you want to send me an affirmation or a message, I would appreciate getting your personal thoughts. Connect with me on Instagram or send me an email. My website www.johnhdaviswriter.com has my blog where I write articles and post veteran resources.

Veterans don't always have the easiest road but it's a better journey if we walk together.

CONCLUSION

Thank you for reading and thank you for your service. Don't let your PTSD win.

John H Davis
www.johnhdaviswriter.com
IG: John.h.davis.writer

Afterward

By Dr. Jessie Virga, USN

The journey of a veteran is a testament to resilience, sacrifice, and unparalleled courage. Each chapter of this book has been a beacon, illuminating the path of healing and self-discovery. The affirmations within these pages are more than just words; they are a call to action, a reminder of the indomitable spirit that resides within every veteran.

The battles faced in uniform are unique, but so too are the battles faced upon returning home. The weight of memories, experiences, and transitions can be overwhelming. Yet, it's essential to remember that the same strength that carried you through the most challenging terrains can guide you through the maze of civilian life.

Affirmations serve as a compass, pointing towards hope, healing, and self-belief. They are not a panacea, but a tool—a daily ritual to center oneself, to reclaim one's narrative, and to harness the power of positive self-talk. The military might have left its mark, but it's the unwavering spirit of service, camaraderie, and resilience that defines a veteran.

As you've journeyed through this book, embracing each affirmation, you've taken steps towards a brighter, more empowered future. The path to healing and self-discovery is ongoing, and while challenges may arise, the tools to face them are now firmly in your grasp. To every veteran who has turned these pages: Your journey,

AFTERWARD

both in uniform and beyond, is a testament to your strength and resilience. May these affirmations serve not just as words, but as a daily reminder of your worth, your potential, and the bright horizon that awaits.

Bio of Dr. Jessie Virga

A proud military veteran, Jessie devoted nearly a decade to honorable service in the U.S. Navy. She's an entrepreneur, owning Mulier Bellator Security, Mulier Bellator Fitness and Valkyrie Nutrition. Dr. Virga is the CEO of Entrepreneur Headquarters. Jessie holds a PhD in Health Psychology and a Doctorate of Business in Homeland Security. She's the author of *The End of Dieting: The Science and Psychology of Sustainable Weight Loss, Building Lean Muscle, and Improving Overall Health.* Guided by her mantra, "uplift and be uplifted," Jessie continues to serve her country and fellow veterans. Follow her fitness and entrepreneur journey @DrVirga on Instagram.

More by the Author

JOHN H DAVIS

COMBAT TO COLLEGE

Applying the Military Mentality as a Student Veteran

MORE BY THE AUTHOR

STUDENT VETERAN
SEMESTER JOURNAL

BY JOHN HOWES DAVIS
AUTHOR OF COMBAT TO COLLEGE

MORE BY THE AUTHOR

Featuring Workouts Submitted By Combat Veterans, NCAA Athletes, NFL Players, WWE Champions, Professional Fighters, Fitness Competitors, And Paralympians...

#FREEDOM CHALLENGE

90 DAYS TO YOUR PERSONAL BEST

Created By

Combat Veteran John H Davis
NFL Veteran Pat Angerer

MORE BY THE AUTHOR

My ten positive affirmations unique to me

1. _____
2. _____
3. _____
4. _____
5. _____
6. _____
7. _____
8. _____
9. _____
10. _____

I'd love to see the veteran affirmations you come up with. If I do a second edition, I'll include them.

Once again, I'm grateful for you.

Your friend,

John